EASY POP MELODIES
FOR BASS

ISBN 978-1-4803-8438-5

HAL•LEONARD®
CORPORATION

7777 W. BLUEMOUND RD. P.O. BOX 13819 MILWAUKEE, WI 53213

ALL MY LOVING

BASS

Words and Music by JOHN LENNON
and PAUL McCARTNEY

BEAUTY AND THE BEAST

from Walt Disney's BEAUTY AND THE BEAST

Lyrics by HOWARD ASHMAN
Music by ALAN MENKEN

Bass

Moderately slow

Tale as old as time, true as it can be.
Tale as old as time, tune as old as song.

Bare-ly e-ven friends, then some bod-y bends un-ex-pect-ed-ly.
Bit-ter-sweet and strange, find-ing you can change, learn-ing you were wrong.

Just a lit-tle change; small, to say the least. Both a lit-tle
Cer-tain as the sun ris-ing in the east. Tale as old as

To Coda

scared, nei-ther one pre-pared, Beau-ty and the Beast. Ev-er just the
time, song as old as rhyme, Beau-ty and the

same, ev-er a sur-prise, ev-er as be-

D.C. al Coda   CODA

fore, ev-er just as sure as the sun will rise.   Beast.

Tale as old as time, song as old as rhyme, Beau-ty and the Beast.

BLOWIN' IN THE WIND

BASS

Words and Music by
BOB DYLAN

Moderately

How man - y roads must a man walk___ down be -
How man - y years can a moun - tain ex - ist be -

fore you call him a man?
fore it is washed to the sea?

How man - y seas must a white dove___ sail be -
How man - y years can some peo - ple ex - ist be -

fore she sleeps in the sand?
fore they're al - lowed to be free?

How man - y times must the can - non - balls___ fly be -
How man - y times can a man turn his head and pre -

fore they're for - ev - er banned? }
tend that he just does - n't see? }

The

an - swer, my friend, is blow - in' in the wind. The

an - swer is blow - in' in the wind.

CAN YOU FEEL THE LOVE TONIGHT
from Walt Disney Pictures' THE LION KING

Music by ELTON JOHN
Lyrics by TIM RICE

CAN'T HELP FALLING IN LOVE

BASS

Words and Music by GEORGE DAVID WEISS,
HUGO PERETTI and LUIGI CREATORE

CLOCKS

Words and Music by GUY BERRYMAN,
JON BUCKLAND, WILL CHAMPION
and CHRIS MARTIN

DAYDREAM BELIEVER

Words and Music by
JOHN STEWART

DON'T KNOW WHY

Words and Music by
JESSE HARRIS

DON'T STOP BELIEVIN'

BASS

Words and Music by STEVE PERRY,
NEAL SCHON and JONATHAN CAIN

EDELWEISS
from THE SOUND OF MUSIC

Lyrics by OSCAR HAMMERSTEIN II
Music by RICHARD RODGERS

BASS

EIGHT DAYS A WEEK

BASS

Words and Music by JOHN LENNON
and PAUL McCARTNEY

Moderately fast

1., 3. Ooh, I need your love, babe; guess you know it's true.
2. Love you ev - 'ry day, girl; al - ways on my mind.

Hope you need my love, babe, just like I need you.
One thing I can say, girl: love you all the time.

Hold me, ___ love me, ___ hold me, ___ love me. ___

Ain't got noth - in' but love, babe, eight days a week. _____

Eight days a week I love _____ you.

Eight days a week is not e - nough to show I care. _

EVERY BREATH YOU TAKE

BASS

Music and Lyrics by
STING

Moderately

N.C.
Ev - 'ry breath you __ take,
Ev - 'ry move you __ make,

Bb
ev - 'ry move you __ make,
ev - 'ry vow you __ break,

Gm

Eb
ev - 'ry bond you break, ev - 'ry step you take, I'll be watch - ing you.
ev - 'ry smile you fake, ev - 'ry claim you stake, I'll be watch - ing you.

F

Gm

Fine

Bb
Ev - 'ry sin - gle __ day,

ev - 'ry word you __ say,

Gm

Eb
ev - 'ry game you play, ev - 'ry night you stay, I'll be watch - ing you.

F

Bb

Oh, can't you __ see

you be - long to __ me?

Eb

Bb

C
How my poor heart __ aches __

with ev - 'ry step __ you take.

F

D.C. al Fine

FIREFLIES

BASS

Words and Music by
ADAM YOUNG

GEORGIA ON MY MIND

Words by STUART GORRELL
Music by HOAGY CARMICHAEL

IN MY LIFE

BASS

Words and Music by JOHN LENNON
and PAUL McCARTNEY

HEY, SOUL SISTER

Words and Music by PAT MONAHAN, ESPEN LIND and AMUND BJORKLAND

HOT N COLD

Words and Music by KATY PERRY,
MAX MARTIN and LUKASZ GOTTWALD

ISN'T SHE LOVELY

Bass

Words and Music by
STEVIE WONDER

THE LETTER

Bass

Words and Music by
WAYNE CARSON THOMPSON

Moderately

Dm **Bb** **C**

1., 3. Give me a tick - et for an aer - o - plane.   Ain't got time __ to take a
2. I don't care how much mon - ey I got - ta spend.   Got to get back __ to my

G **Dm** **Bb**

fast __ train. }
ba - by again. }   Lone - ly days are gone; __   I'm a - go - in' home. __ Oh, my

A   1. **Dm**   **Fine**   2. **Dm**

ba - by just wrote me a let - ter.   - ter.

F **C** **Bb** **F**

Well, she wrote __ me a let - ter, said she could - n't live __ with - out __

C **F** **C**

__ me no more.   Lis - ten, mis - ter, can't you see I

Bb **F** **C** **A**

D.C. al Fine
(take 1st ending)

got to get back __ to my ba - by once more?   An - y - way, __ yeah.

LIKE A VIRGIN

BASS

Words and Music by BILLY STEINBERG
and TOM KELLY

Moderately

I made it through the wil - der - ness. Some - how I made it through. _____
all my love, _ boy. _ My fear is fad - ing fast. _____

Did - n't know how lost _____ I was _____ un - til I
Been _ sav - ing it all for you _____ 'cause on - ly

_____ found you. _____ I was beat, _____ in - com - plete. _____ I'd been had; _____
love can last. _____ You're so fine _____ and you're mine. _____ Make me strong; _

_____ I was sad _____ and blue. _ But you made me feel, _____
_____ yeah, you make _ me bold. _ Oh, your loved thawed out, _____

yeah, you made _____ me feel _____ shin - y and new. _
yeah, your love thawed out _____ what was scared _ and cold. _

_____ Like a vir - gin touched for the
_____ Like a vir - gin touched for the

ver - y first time. Like a vir - gin _____ when your
ver - y first time. Like a vir - gin _____ with your

heart beats next to _____ mine. _ Gonna give you
heart - beat next to _____ mine. _

THE LOOK OF LOVE

from CASINO ROYALE

BASS

Words by HAL DAVID
Music by BURT BACHARACH

LOVE ME TENDER

Words and Music by ELVIS PRESLEY
and VERA MATSON

BASS

MR. TAMBOURINE MAN

BASS

Words and Music by
BOB DYLAN

LOVE STORY

BASS

Words and Music by
TAYLOR SWIFT

MOON RIVER

from the Paramount Picture BREAKFAST AT TIFFANY'S

Words by JOHNNY MERCER
Music by HENRY MANCINI

Bass

MORNING HAS BROKEN

BASS

Words by ELEANOR FARJEON
Music by CAT STEVENS

MY CHERIE AMOUR

BASS

Words and Music by STEVIE WONDER,
SYLVIA MOY and HENRY COSBY

MY GIRL

BASS

Words and Music by WILLIAM "SMOKEY" ROBINSON
and RONALD WHITE

MY FAVORITE THINGS

from THE SOUND OF MUSIC

BASS

Lyrics by OSCAR HAMMERSTEIN II
Music by RICHARD RODGERS

MY HEART WILL GO ON
(Love Theme from 'Titanic')
from the Paramount and Twentieth Century Fox Motion Picture TITANIC

Music by JAMES HORNER
Lyric by WILL JENNINGS

Bass

NIGHTS IN WHITE SATIN

Words and Music by
JUSTIN HAYWARD

BASS

NOWHERE MAN

BASS

Words and Music by JOHN LENNON
and PAUL McCARTNEY

PUFF THE MAGIC DRAGON

Words and Music by LENNY LIPTON
and PETER YARROW

BASS

RAINDROPS KEEP FALLIN' ON MY HEAD

from BUTCH CASSIDY AND THE SUNDANCE KID

Lyric by HAL DAVID
Music by BURT BACHARACH

BASS

SCARBOROUGH FAIR/CANTICLE

BASS

Arrangement and Original Counter Melody by PAUL SIMON
and ARTHUR GARFUNKEL

SOMEWHERE OUT THERE

from AN AMERICAN TAIL

Music by BARRY MANN and JAMES HORNER
Lyric by CYNTHIA WEIL

BASS

THE SOUND OF MUSIC
from THE SOUND OF MUSIC

BASS

Lyrics by OSCAR HAMMERSTEIN II
Music by RICHARD RODGERS

STRANGERS IN THE NIGHT

adapted from A MAN COULD GET KILLED

Bass

Words by CHARLES SINGLETON and EDDIE SNYDER
Music by BERT KAEMPFERT

SUNSHINE ON MY SHOULDERS

Words by JOHN DENVER
Music by JOHN DENVER, MIKE TAYLOR
and DICK KNISS

Bass

SWEET CAROLINE

Words and Music by
NEIL DIAMOND

TILL THERE WAS YOU
from Meredith Willson's THE MUSIC MAN

Bass

By MEREDITH WILLSON

THE TIMES THEY ARE A-CHANGIN'

BASS

Words and Music by
BOB DYLAN

Moderately fast

Come gath - er 'round, peo - ple, wher - ev - er you roam,
writ - ers and crit - ics who prophe - size with your pen,

and ad - mit that the wa - ters a - round you have
and keep your eyes wide; the chance won't come a -

grown, and ac - cept it that soon you'll be drenched to the
gain. And don't speak too soon, for the wheel's still in

bone. If your time to you is worth
spin. And there's no tell - in' who that it's

sav - in', then you bet - ter start swim - ming or you'll
nam - in', for the los - er now will be

sink like a stone,⎫ for the times, they are a -
lat - er to win, ⎭

1.
2.

chang - in'. Come

UNCHAINED MELODY

BASS

Lyric by HY ZARET
Music by ALEX NORTH

TOMORROW
from The Musical Production ANNIE

Lyric by MARTIN CHARNIN
Music by CHARLES STROUSE

VIVA LA VIDA

Words and Music by GUY BERRYMAN,
JON BUCKLAND, WILL CHAMPION
and CHRIS MARTIN

BASS

Moderately

I used to rule the world. ___ Seas would rise when I gave the word. ___

___ Now in the morn-ing I sleep a - lone, ___ sweep the

streets I used to own. ___

I used to roll the dice, ___ feel the

fear in my en-e-my's eyes, ___ lis-ten as the crowd ___ would sing, ___

___ "Now the old king is dead; ___ long live the king." One min-ute I

held the key, ___ next the walls were closed on

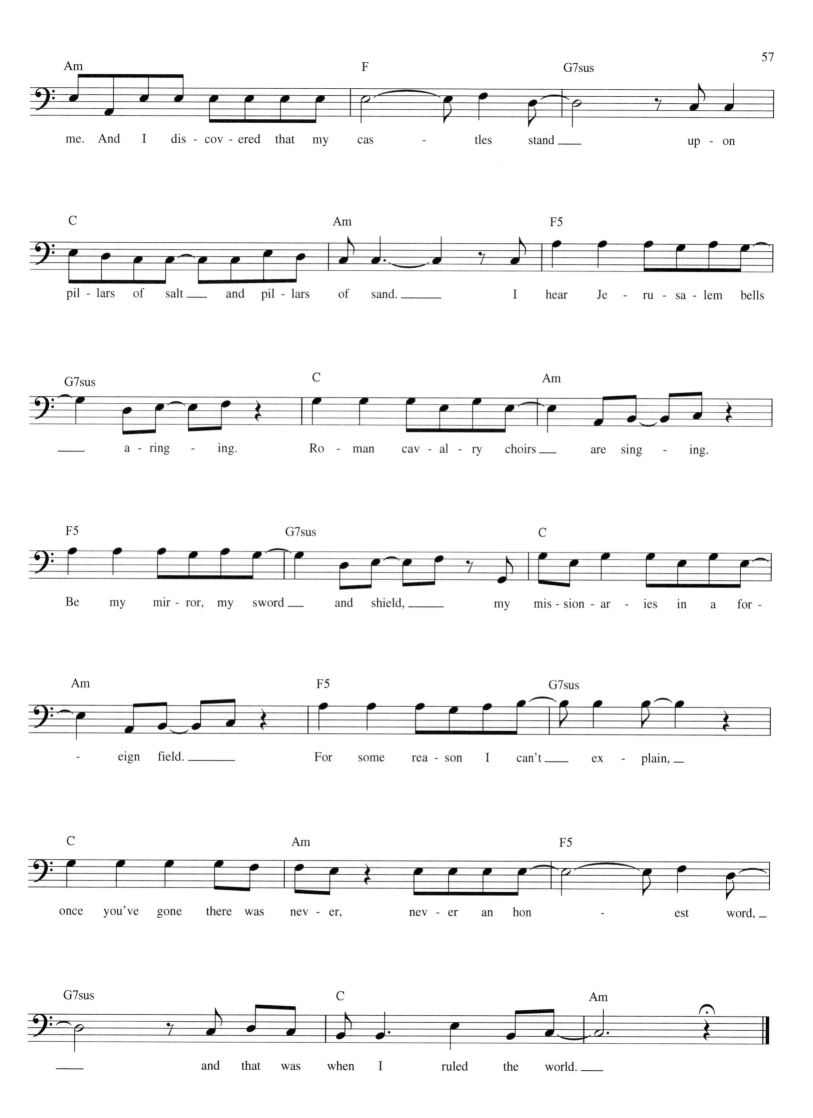

WE ARE THE WORLD

BASS

Words and Music by LIONEL RICHIE
and MICHAEL JACKSON

WHAT A WONDERFUL WORLD

Bass

Words and Music by GEORGE DAVID WEISS
and BOB THIELE

Moderately slow

I see trees of green, red ros-es too. I see them bloom
skies of blue and clouds of white, the bright blessed day,
ba-bies cry; I watch them grow. They'll learn much more

for me and you.
the dark sacred night. And I think to my-self:___ What a won-der-ful
than I'll ever know.

1. C F#9b5 Fmaj7 G7
world!_____ I see

2. C Dm/C C
world!_____ The

F/G G7 Cmaj7 C6 F/G G7
col-ors of the rain-bow, so pret-ty in the sky, are al-so on the fac-es of

Cmaj7 C6 Am G/B Am G
peo-ple go-ing by. I see friends shak-ing hands, say-ing, "How do you do?"

Am C#dim7 Dm7 G7
They're real-ly say-ing, "I love you." I hear

D.S. al Coda

CODA

C Bb7b5 A9 A7b9 A7
world!_____ I

Dm7 G7b9 C Dm/C C
think to my-self:___ What a won-der-ful world!_____

WONDERWALL

Words and Music by
NOEL GALLAGHER

YOU ARE THE SUNSHINE OF MY LIFE

Bass

Words and Music by
STEVIE WONDER

Brightly

You are the sun - shine of __ my life. __
You are the ap - ple of __ my eye. __

That's why I'll al - ways be __ a - round. __
For - ev - er you'll __ stay in __ my heart. __

I feel like this __ is the __ be - gin - ning, __

though I've loved you __ for a thou - sand years. __

And if I thought __ our love __ was end - ing, __ I'd find __

__ my - self __ drown - ing in my __ own tears. Whoa, __ whoa. __

YOU'VE GOT A FRIEND

BASS

Words and Music by
CAROLE KING

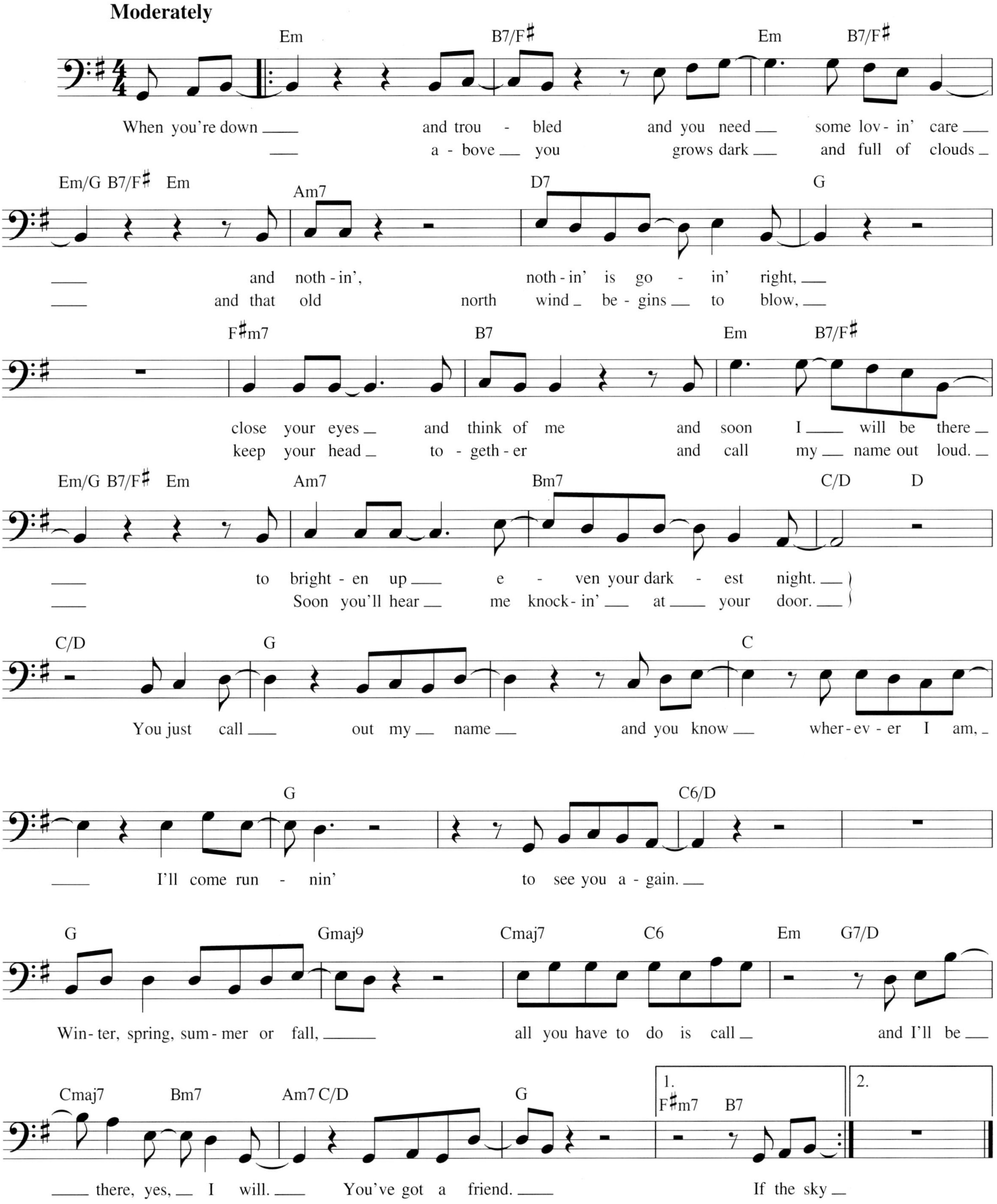

HAL•LEONARD INSTRUMENTAL PLAY-ALONG

Your favorite songs are arranged just for solo instrumentalists with this outstanding series. Each book includes great full-accompaniment play-along audio so you can sound just like a pro!

Check out **halleonard.com** for songlists and more titles!

12 Pop Hits
12 songs
00261790	Flute	00261795	Horn
00261791	Clarinet	00261796	Trombone
00261792	Alto Sax	00261797	Violin
00261793	Tenor Sax	00261798	Viola
00261794	Trumpet	00261799	Cello

The Very Best of Bach
15 selections
00225371	Flute	00225376	Horn
00225372	Clarinet	00225377	Trombone
00225373	Alto Sax	00225378	Violin
00225374	Tenor Sax	00225379	Viola
00225375	Trumpet	00225380	Cello

The Beatles
15 songs
00225330	Flute	00225335	Horn
00225331	Clarinet	00225336	Trombone
00225332	Alto Sax	00225337	Violin
00225333	Tenor Sax	00225338	Viola
00225334	Trumpet	00225339	Cello

Chart Hits
12 songs
00146207	Flute	00146212	Horn
00146208	Clarinet	00146213	Trombone
00146209	Alto Sax	00146214	Violin
00146210	Tenor Sax	00146211	Trumpet
00146216	Cello		

Christmas Songs
12 songs
00146855	Flute	00146863	Horn
00146858	Clarinet	00146864	Trombone
00146859	Alto Sax	00146866	Violin
00146860	Tenor Sax	00146867	Viola
00146862	Trumpet	00146868	Cello

Contemporary Broadway
15 songs
00298704	Flute	00298709	Horn
00298705	Clarinet	00298710	Trombone
00298706	Alto Sax	00298711	Violin
00298707	Tenor Sax	00298712	Viola
00298708	Trumpet	00298713	Cello

Disney Movie Hits
12 songs
00841420	Flute	00841424	Horn
00841687	Oboe	00841425	Trombone
00841421	Clarinet	00841426	Violin
00841422	Alto Sax	00841427	Viola
00841686	Tenor Sax	00841428	Cello
00841423	Trumpet		

Prices, contents, and availability subject to change without notice.

Disney characters and artwork ™ & © 2021 Disney

Disney Solos
12 songs
00841404	Flute	00841506	Oboe
00841406	Alto Sax	00841409	Trumpet
00841407	Horn	00841410	Violin
00841411	Viola	00841412	Cello
00841405	Clarinet/Tenor Sax		
00841408	Trombone/Baritone		
00841553	Mallet Percussion		

Dixieland Favorites
15 songs
00268756	Flute	0068759	Trumpet
00268757	Clarinet	00268760	Trombone
00268758	Alto Sax		

Billie Eilish
9 songs
00345648	Flute	00345653	Horn
00345649	Clarinet	00345654	Trombone
00345650	Alto Sax	00345655	Violin
00345651	Tenor Sax	00345656	Viola
00345652	Trumpet	00345657	Cello

Favorite Movie Themes
13 songs
00841166	Flute	00841168	Trumpet
00841167	Clarinet	00841170	Trombone
00841169	Alto Sax	00841296	Violin

Gospel Hymns
15 songs
00194648	Flute	00194654	Trombone
00194649	Clarinet	00194655	Violin
00194650	Alto Sax	00194656	Viola
00194651	Tenor Sax	00194657	Cello
00194652	Trumpet		

Great Classical Themes
15 songs
00292727	Flute	00292733	Horn
00292728	Clarinet	00292735	Trombone
00292729	Alto Sax	00292736	Violin
00292730	Tenor Sax	00292737	Viola
00292732	Trumpet	00292738	Cello

The Greatest Showman
8 songs
00277389	Flute	00277394	Horn
00277390	Clarinet	00277395	Trombone
00277391	Alto Sax	00277396	Violin
00277392	Tenor Sax	00277397	Viola
00277393	Trumpet	00277398	Cello

Irish Favorites
31 songs
00842489	Flute	00842495	Trombone
00842490	Clarinet	00842496	Violin
00842491	Alto Sax	00842497	Viola
00842493	Trumpet	00842498	Cello
00842494	Horn		

Michael Jackson
11 songs
00119495	Flute	00119499	Trumpet
00119496	Clarinet	00119501	Trombone
00119497	Alto Sax	00119503	Violin
00119498	Tenor Sax	00119502	Accomp.

Jazz & Blues
14 songs
00841438	Flute	00841441	Trumpet
00841439	Clarinet	00841443	Trombone
00841440	Alto Sax	00841444	Violin
00841442	Tenor Sax		

Jazz Classics
12 songs
00151812	Flute	00151816	Trumpet
00151813	Clarinet	00151818	Trombone
00151814	Alto Sax	00151819	Violin
00151815	Tenor Sax	00151821	Cello

Les Misérables
13 songs
00842292	Flute	00842297	Horn
00842293	Clarinet	00842298	Trombone
00842294	Alto Sax	00842299	Violin
00842295	Tenor Sax	00842300	Viola
00842296	Trumpet	00842301	Cello

Metallica
12 songs
02501327	Flute	02502454	Horn
02501339	Clarinet	02501329	Trombone
02501332	Alto Sax	02501334	Violin
02501333	Tenor Sax	02501335	Viola
02501330	Trumpet	02501338	Cello

Motown Classics
15 songs
00842572	Flute	00842576	Trumpet
00842573	Clarinet	00842578	Trombone
00842574	Alto Sax	00842579	Violin
00842575	Tenor Sax		

Pirates of the Caribbean
16 songs
00842183	Flute	00842188	Horn
00842184	Clarinet	00842189	Trombone
00842185	Alto Sax	00842190	Violin
00842186	Tenor Sax	00842191	Viola
00842187	Trumpet	00842192	Cello

Queen
17 songs
00285402	Flute	00285407	Horn
00285403	Clarinet	00285408	Trombone
00285404	Alto Sax	00285409	Violin
00285405	Tenor Sax	00285410	Viola
00285406	Trumpet	00285411	Cello

Simple Songs
14 songs
00249081	Flute	00249087	Horn
00249093	Oboe	00249089	Trombone
00249082	Clarinet	00249090	Violin
00249083	Alto Sax	00249091	Viola
00249084	Tenor Sax	00249092	Cello
00249086	Trumpet	00249094	Mallets

Superhero Themes
14 songs
00363195	Flute	00363200	Horn
00363196	Clarinet	00363201	Trombone
00363197	Alto Sax	00363202	Violin
00363198	Tenor Sax	00363203	Viola
00363199	Trumpet	00363204	Cello

Star Wars
16 songs
00350900	Flute	00350907	Horn
00350913	Oboe	00350908	Trombone
00350903	Clarinet	00350909	Violin
00350904	Alto Sax	00350910	Viola
00350905	Tenor Sax	00350911	Cello
00350906	Trumpet	00350914	Mallet

Taylor Swift
15 songs
00842532	Flute	00842537	Horn
00842533	Clarinet	00842538	Trombone
00842534	Alto Sax	00842539	Violin
00842535	Tenor Sax	00842540	Viola
00842536	Trumpet	00842541	Cello

Video Game Music
13 songs
00283877	Flute	00283883	Horn
00283878	Clarinet	00283884	Trombone
00283879	Alto Sax	00283885	Violin
00283880	Tenor Sax	00283886	Viola
00283882	Trumpet	00283887	Cello

Wicked
13 songs
00842236	Flute	00842241	Horn
00842237	Clarinet	00842242	Trombone
00842238	Alto Sax	00842243	Violin
00842239	Tenor Sax	00842244	Viola
00842240	Trumpet	00842245	Cello

HAL•LEONARD®

0122
488